CONTENTS

1.1 Types of Sources

Historians and sources

Historians are people who like history and want to find out about the past. They look for all sorts of things that tell them about the past. Sources are the things that tell historians about the past. There are many different kinds of sources.

castles

books

weapons

pottery

Primary sources

Primary sources come from the time that historians are studying.

Secondary sources

Secondary sources usually come from later than the time historians are studying.

The Middle Ages

The Middle Ages is the name given to the time from 1066 to 1500. The Middle Ages is also called the Medieval period.

A

SOURCE

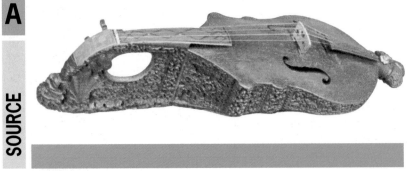

A medieval musical instrument.

C

SOURCE

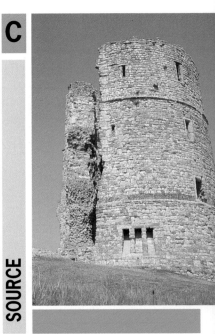

Hadleigh Castle, built in 1232.

Foundation History

THE MEDIEVAL REALMS

Fiona Reynoldson

KELMSCOTT SCHOOL
MARKHOUSE ROAD
WALTHAMSTOW., LONDON E17 8DN
TEL AND FAX: 0181 5212115

Heinemann

Heinemann Educational Publishers
Halley Court, Jordan Hill, Oxford OX2 8EJ
a division of Reed Educational & Professional
Publishing Ltd

OXFORD MELBOURNE AUCKLAND
CHICAGO PORTSMOUTH (NH) BLANTYRE
IBADAN GABORONE JOHANNESBURG

© Fiona Reynoldson

The moral right of the proprietors has been asserted

First published 1994

**British Library Cataloguing in Publication Data is available
from the Brirish Library on request.**

ISBN 0-435-31682-6

99 98

10 9 8 7

Designed by Ron Kamen, Green Door Design Ltd,
Basingstoke

Illustrated by Jeff Edwards Douglas Hall Peter Hicks
Stuart Hughes Terry Thomas

Printed in Hong Kong by Wing King Tong Co. Ltd.

The front cover shows: Villeins being attacked by Brigands

Acknowledgements

The author and publisher would like to thank the following
for permission to reproduce photographs:

Bibliothèque National: 4.1B, 4.2B, 4.7E, 5.1C
Bibliothèque Royale Albert, Brussels: 5.2C
Bodleian Library: 3.8A, 4.2B, 5.1C
British Library: Cover, 3.2B, C, D and E, 3.8B, 4.1A, 4.2A
and D, 4.3B, 4.4B, 4.5A and B, 4.6B, 4.7D and F, 4.8A and D,
5.3F, 5.4A and E
The Trustees of the British Museum: 1.1A
Cadw: Welsh Historic Monuments. Crown Copyright: 3.7C
Cambridge University Library: 4.8B
Cambridge University Technical Services Ltd: 2.5C
J. Allan Cash Ltd: 1.1C
The Dean and Chapter of Durham: 2.4B
Mary Evans Picture Library: 4.9D
English Heritage: 2.6A
Giraudon: 4.6A
Sonia Halliday Photographs: 3.3C
Hastings Tourism and Leisure Department: 3.4B
Michael Holford: 1.1D, 2.1A, 2.2A and B
Lauros-Giraudon: 4.7A
Mansell Collection: 2.3C
Sealand Aerial Photography: 2.5A
Source Photographic Archives: 3.6D
Trinity College, Cambridge: 4.4A, 4.5C, D and E

Woodsmansterne Ltd/Nicholas Servian: 4.3A
Source 3.5A is reproduced from a former edition of the
Ladybird title *Kings and Queens Volume I*, illustrated by Frank
Hampson with permission of the publishers, Ladybird Books
Ltd.

Every effort has been made to contact copyright holders of
material reproduced in this book. Any omissions will be
rectified in subsequent printings if notice is given to the
publisher.

Details of Written Sources

In some sources the wording or sentence structure has been
simplified to ensure that the source is accessible.

R. Barber, *A Strong Land and a Sturdy*, Deutsch, 1976: 4.8F
Norman Cohn, The Pursuit of the Millennium, Paladin,
1970: 3.3A
G. G. Coulton, *Medieval Panorama II: The Horizons of
Thought*, Cambridge University Press, 1938: 4.8E
C. Culpin, *Past Into Present 1*, Collins Educational, 1988:
5.1D
R. B. Dobson, *The Peasants Revolt of 1381*, Macmillan, 1970:
5.3A, B, C, D and E, 5.4B, C and D
A. A. Erskine and A. L. Davidson, *Scotland at Peace, At War,
1263–1329*, Edward Arnold, 1978: 3.8C
G. N. Garmonsway (Trans.), *The Anglo-Saxon Chronicle*, J. M.
Dent & Sons Ltd, 1953: 2.7A
J. A. Giles (Ed.) *William of Malmesbury's Chronicle of the Kings
of England*, Henry Bohun, 1847: 2.3B
Elizabeth Hallam (Ed.), *Chronicles of the Crusades: Eye-
Witness Accounts of the Wars Between Christianity and Islam*,
Weidenfeld and Nicolson, 1989: 3.3B and D
Heritage of Britain, Readers Digest Association, 1975: 3.7B
Jean Marx (Ed.), *Guillaume de Jumieges, Gesta Normannorum
Ducum*, Societé de L'Histoire de Normandie, 1914: 2.2C
T. W. Moody and F. X. Matin (Eds.), *The Course of Irish
History*, Mercier Press, 1967: 3.6A, B and C
Peter Moss, *History Alive*, Hart Davis Educational Ltd, 1977:
3.1A
L. du Garde Peach, *The Kings and Queens of England*, Ladybird
Books, 1968: 3.5A
D. Richards and A. D. Ellis, *Medieval Britain*, Longman, 1973:
3.4A, 3.7A, 5.2A
Schools Council Project: History 13–16, *Medicine Through
Time 2: The Beginning of Change*, Holmes McDougall, 1976:
4.8C, 5.1G
Paul Shuter and John Child, *Skills in History 1: Changes*,
Heinemann Educational, 1987: 1.1B
L. E. Snellgrove, *The Early Modern Age*, Longman, 1972: 4.9B
David Whitehall, *Life in Norman Times*, Edward Arnold,
1989: 2.3A, 2.4A, 3.1C and 4.2C

D

SOURCE

Questions

1 Look at the dates below. Write down the right dates for the Medieval period:

      1966–2000
      1000–1566
      1066–1500

Read **Historians and sources**, **Primary sources** (look at the pictures) and **Secondary sources**.

2 Fill in the gaps. Use the words in the box.

Sources are things that tell historians about the _____.

A primary source comes from the _____ that you are studying.

A secondary source comes from a _____ time.

> later   past   time

3 Write down two headings: **Primary Sources** and **Secondary Sources**. Look at the sources on pages 4 and 5. Which are primary sources? Which are secondary sources? Write the letter of each source under the right heading.

Part of the Bayeux Tapestry (made in about 1080). This scene shows the Normans and the English fighting.

E

SOURCE

A modern school textbook, printed in 1991.

2.1 Why was there an Invasion?

England up for grabs

King Edward the Confessor died in 1066. He had no children. So who was to be the next king? Three men wanted to be king.

Harold Godwinson of England

Harold Godwinson was the most powerful man in England. His sister was married to King Edward the Confessor. Just before he died, Edward the Confessor had said Harold should be king. Many of the rich, powerful men in England wanted Harold to be king. So Harold was crowned king.

King Harald Hardrada of Norway

But King Harald Hardrada of Norway wanted to be king too. He was a powerful king with a big army and he liked the idea of being king of a rich country like England. He was related to King Canute, who had been King of England from 1016–35. He said he should be king.

Duke William of Normandy

Duke William did not want Harold Godwinson to be king of England. William said Edward the Confessor had promised that William would be king. He said Harold knew about this. He said that Harold had taken an oath to help William become king. Harold said this was not true. True or not, William was angry.

NORWAY

ENGLAND

NORMANDY

Fighting for England.

NORWAY

ENGLAND

NORMANDY

Questions

Read **England up for grabs**.

1 Fill in the gaps. Use the words in the box.
King Edward the Confessor died in _____. Edward had no _____. This made it hard to decide who should be the next _____.

children	1066	king

2 Draw or trace the cartoon on page 7. Write the name of each king next to him. Use the paragraph headings and the map on page 6 to help you name the kings.

A scene from the Bayeux Tapestry. It shows Harold Godwinson swearing to help William. The Tapestry was made by Normans.

A

SOURCE

VBI hAROLD:SACRAMENTVM:FECIT: hIC hA VVILLELMO DVCI:

2.2 The Norman Victory

Halley's Comet, 1066

In 1066, people saw a bright comet in the night sky. They shook their heads. They said it was a bad sign. It was. By the end of the year two armies had come to invade England. Two kings were dead.

King Harald Hardrada of Norway

First King Harald Hardrada sailed to England with a huge fleet of ships filled with soldiers. The soldiers rushed from the ships and defeated the English at the Battle of Fulford.

King Harold of England marches north

Harold marched north and beat Harald's army at the Battle of Stamford Bridge. Harald Hardrada was killed, together with thousands of his men. It was 25 September, 1066.

King Harold of England marches south

However, Harold could not stay in the north to celebrate his victory. A messenger arrived. He said that Duke William of Normandy had landed in England and there was no one to stop him. Harold got his tired soldiers together and marched south.

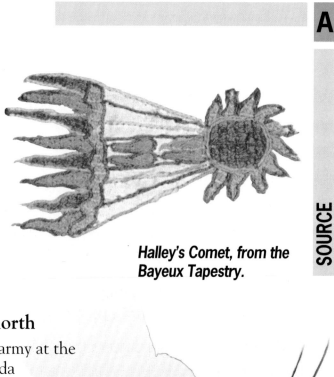

Halley's Comet, from the Bayeux Tapestry.

—— Hardrada

—— Harold

—— William

York
× × Stamford Bridge
× Fulford
R. Humber
NORTH SE

Hardrada and Tostig land with invasion fleet

ENGLAND

Harold marches north to face Hardrada

Harold marches south to face William

R. Thames
● London

× Hastings
Pevensey ●

William lands at Pevensey

● St Vale

ENGLISH CHANNEL

NORMANDY

Bayeux ●

The Battle of Hastings

It was the night of 13 October, 1066. Harold reached Hastings. He had about 7000 soldiers. He had no time to send messengers to get more soldiers. The next morning William's scouts rode out and saw the English army on the hills beyond Hastings. William set out his army of crossbowmen, archers and cavalry in the valley. Harold's army was crowded on the hill above.

The battle raged all day. Again and again the Normans charged on horseback up the hill. Again and again the English forced them back. At last the Normans pretended to run away. The English ran down the hill after them. But the Normans were not running away. They turned their horses and cut down the English soldiers.

By nightfall Harold was dead and William had won the battle. Who could stop him being king now?

 Death of King Harold

Written by a Norman monk in 1070.

Questions

Read **King Harald Hardrada of Norway** and **King Harold of England marches north**.

1 Copy the sentences below. Choose one of the words in *italics* each time there is a choice.
Harald Hardrada came from *Norway/China*. His soldiers beat the *French/English*. King Harold heard about this. He marched his army *south/east*.

2 Write a sentence about what happened at Stamford Bridge.

3 Write a sentence saying who won the Battle of Hastings.

B

SOURCE

The Normans preparing to invade England. From the Bayeux Tapestry.

2.3 The Victory Completed

What did the English do?

William of Normandy had beaten the English army. He had killed the English king. What would the English do? William waited. The English did nothing. So William captured Dover. Then he captured Canterbury. Then he captured Winchester. Still the English did nothing. So William marched towards London. He watched all the time for signs of trouble.

King of England

It was December 1066. William marched into the city of London. On Christmas Day he was crowned king of England in Westminster Abbey.

The North

But not everyone wanted William to be king. Many people in the north of England rebelled.

Help for the rebels

The king of Denmark sent soldiers to help them and they burnt William's castle in York. William was furious. He sent soldiers to fight the rebels. Then he ordered his soldiers to burn farms and villages and kill animals all around York. This was to teach the people of the north a lesson.

Hereward

Some people still hated William and the Normans. One of these people was Hereward. He led many English rebels in an area called the Fens (see map on this page). These people knew the safe paths through the wet, marshy Fens and often they hid on the islands.

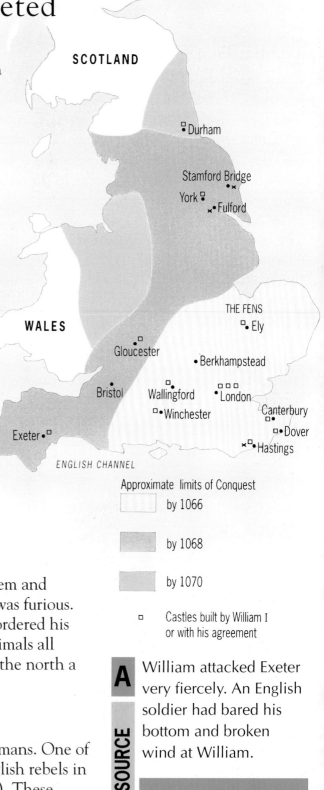

Approximate limits of Conquest

by 1066

by 1068

by 1070

□ Castles built by William I or with his agreement

A William attacked Exeter very fiercely. An English soldier had bared his bottom and broken wind at William.

SOURCE

Written by an English monk in 1120.

It was difficult for William's soldiers to follow. In the end, someone led the Normans along a safe path through the marshes to the island of Ely. The Normans captured Ely in 1071. That was the end of the English rebellions against the Normans, although Hereward was never caught.

B

SOURCE

People were so hungry they ate human flesh, horses, cats and dogs. There was a terrible smell because no one was alive to bury the dead. For nine years no one lived in the villages between York and Durham.

An English monk describes William's punishment of the English rebels. This was written about fifty years later.

A picture from the 19th century showing Hereward fighting the Normans.

C

SOURCE

Questions

Read **What did the English do?** and **King of England.**

1 Read the sentences below. Copy out the true ones.

William beat the English army.

King Harold hid in Wales.

William marched to Dover.

The soldiers went swimming.

William captured Dover, Canterbury and Winchester.

William was crowned king on Christmas Day, 1066.

Look at the map on page 10.
2 a How many castles are shown on the map?
  b Write a list of all the towns and cities on the map. Write next to each name the year by which it was captured.

Look at Source C.
3 a When was it made?
  b Is it a primary source or a secondary source?
  c Choose two of the words below which you think best describe what the artist thought Hereward was like.

brave   fat   short   strong
heroic   mean   shy   cowardly

  d 'Source C shows us what Hereward was like.' Do you agree or not? Write a sentence to explain why.

2.4 Keeping Control: The Feudal System

William owned England

William said that he had conquered England. He said this meant that all the land in England belonged to him. But William could not look after all of England by himself. So he gave pieces of England to his Norman friends. These friends were called lords, barons or tenants-in-chief. They gave smaller pieces of land to knights or under-tenants. The picture on page 13 explains how this worked.

The picture on page 13 explains how this worked.

A **SOURCE**

I become your man from now on. I shall be loyal to you for the lands I hold from you.

The oath taken in Norman times.

What the tenants-in-chief had to do

William gave the tenants-in-chief land to farm. But they had to do two things in return:

1 The tenants-in-chief swore to be William's loyal friends.
2 The tenants-in-chief had to work for William.

Loyalty

Being loyal to William meant that the tenants-in-chief would fight for William against his enemies. They promised not to plot against William with each other or with his enemies.

Working for William

Working for William meant sending him as many soldiers as he asked for. These soldiers fought if William needed them to. If William did not need them to fight, they guarded his castles.

B **SOURCE**

A 13th-century painting. This shows a knight doing homage to the king.

How the feudal system worked.

Questions

Look at the picture on this page.

1 Write a sentence to answer each of the following questions.

   a What did the king give the baron (his tenant-in-chief)?

   b What did the baron do for the king?

   c What job did the under-tenant do for the baron?

   d What did the baron give the under-tenant?

   e Who did the peasant work for?

Read Source A and **Loyalty**.

2 a Write a sentence to say what the tenant-in-chief promised the king in this oath.

   b Do you think that this was as important as sending the king soldiers? Why do you think this?

Look at Source B.

3 Draw a picture of a knight doing homage. It can be a very simple picture. Write a sentence underneath to explain what doing homage was. The words below will help you.

> king   knight   loyal   promise

2.5 Keeping Control: Motte & Bailey Castles

William and his Norman friends

William's powerful Norman friends had fought for him at the Battle of Hastings. William gave them plenty of land in England. Now they had to control the English.

How William kept control of England

William told his Norman friends to build castles as quickly as they could. They had to build them in places where they could control the land all around. Then William told his Norman bishops to build cathedrals in the big towns.

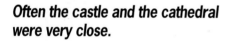

Often the castle and the cathedral were very close.

Controlling the people

William's Norman friends became great lords. They built about 60 motte and bailey castles in England. Norman soldiers could ride 20–30 miles in a half a day. It was easy to ride out from the castles and keep control of the English. They could stop them from turning against the Normans.

A

SOURCE

Carisbrooke Castle. The motte was built around 1070.

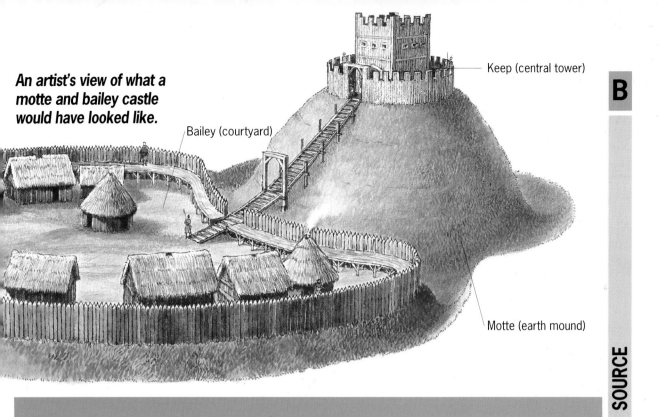

An artist's view of what a motte and bailey castle would have looked like.

Keep (central tower)

Bailey (courtyard)

Motte (earth mound)

You can see the remains of a motte and bailey castle in this photograph which was taken at Pleshey, in Essex.

Questions

1 Read **How William kept control of England**. Copy the sentences below. Choose one of the words in *italics* each time there is a choice. William *did/did not* want to have England taken away from him. He needed the help of his powerful *friends/dogs*. The Normans built *castles/ships*. They built *boats/cathedrals* too. They did this to control the *Americans/English*.

Look at Sources A and B.
2 **a** Which source is a primary source?
   b Write down four differences between the castles in the sources.

2.6 Keeping Control: Square Keep Castles

Wooden castles

Motte and bailey castles were made of wood. They had two big problems:
1 Wooden castles can be burnt down.
2 Wooden castles rot.

Stone castles

Stone castles were much stronger than wooden ones. William encouraged his Norman friends to build stone castles as soon as they could. The castles had huge, thick walls. Sometimes the walls were 4 metres thick. The Normans felt safe in their castles.

Starving the castle

The stone castles were very strong. Soldiers in the castle could hold out for weeks or months if they had enough food. Sometimes an army had to camp all round a castle and just wait until the soldiers inside starved.

Scotland and Wales

Gradually the Norman kings had more and more stone castles built in England. Then they built castles in Scotland and Wales. In this way, William and the Norman kings who came after him, worked hard to control the lands they had conquered.

Rochester Castle, in Kent, is a stone castle with a square keep. The keep is the big tower in the middle of the castle. It was the safest part. Rochester was begun in 1127. It was built for King Henry I.

A

SOURCE

An artist's drawing of a square keep. The lord and his family lived in the keep all the time. Everyone came into the keep if the castle was attacked.

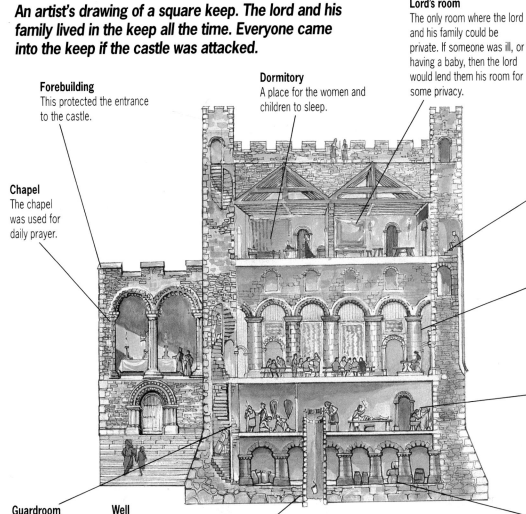

Forebuilding
This protected the entrance to the castle.

Chapel
The chapel was used for daily prayer.

Dormitory
A place for the women and children to sleep.

Lord's room
The only room where the lord and his family could be private. If someone was ill, or having a baby, then the lord would lend them his room for some privacy.

Toilets
The toilets were set above each other, and had a central drain which opened on the outside of the keep. The drains were kept small, so that the attackers could not get in that way.

Great Hall
The largest and most important room in the keep. It was used by everyone for eating and meeting together.

Kitchen
The kitchen was used for very basic cooking. Most keeps had bigger kitchens in the bailey.

Cellars
Food, arms and ammunition were stored in the cellars. Prisoners were kept here, too.

Guardroom
The guardroom was used by off-duty guards.

Well
Keeps were deliberately built in places where there was water for a well, otherwise the defenders could easily have been starved out.

Questions

Read **Wooden castles**.

1 Fill in the gaps. Use the words in the box.
There were two big problems with wooden castles. Wooden castles catch _____ easily and burn down. Wood also _____. Stone castles were much _____.

rots	stronger	fire

Look at the picture on this page.

2 Write down the heading **The Keep**. Copy the sentences about keeps below, matching the Heads and Tails.

The well   was where they went to pray.
The dormitory   protected the entrance.
The Great Hall   was where everyone ate.
The chapel   was for sleeping in.
The forebuilding   was where the water came from.

2.7 The Land the Normans Ruled

Money

William needed money to pay for extra soldiers in case anyone attacked England.

How could William get the money?

William wanted to get the money from everyone living in England. But how much could each person afford to pay? William did not know. So he decided to ask everyone in England.

The Domesday Survey, 1086

William did not ask everyone himself. He sent men all over England. They asked lots of questions. (Look at the picture opposite.) They found out how many pigs, hens, cows, windmills and farm tools everyone had. All the answers were collected up. Now William could work out how much money each person in England could afford to pay him.

The Domesday Book

All the answers were put in a book called The Domesday Book. Copies that were made of The Domesday Book still survive today. One of these is kept in the Public Record Office in London. Historians can go in and use it. It tells historians a lot about England in 1086.

A

SOURCE

Before 1086 in Shipley, Ravenchil owned the land. The village had 2 ploughs.
Value: 10 shillings a year.
Now it is wasteland.

From the Domesday entry for Shipley in Yorkshire.

B

Azor holds Offham from Earl Roger.
There are: 8 villagers
5 cottagers
5 slaves
2 ploughs
a meadow
a fishery, worth
   2 shillings
woodland for 3 pigs.
Value: £4 a year.

From the Domesday entry for Offham in Sussex.

Questions

Read **The Domesday Survey, 1086**.

1 Write this down as a heading. Then copy the sentences below in **chronological** order. That is the order they happened.
   a William knew how much people could pay him.
   b William sent men all over England to ask questions.
   c The answers told William how rich people were.
   d The answers were collected together to make the Domesday Book.

Read Source A and Source B.

2 Would you rather have lived in Offham or Shipley in 1086? Write at least a sentence to explain your reasons.

Types of people living in England in 1086

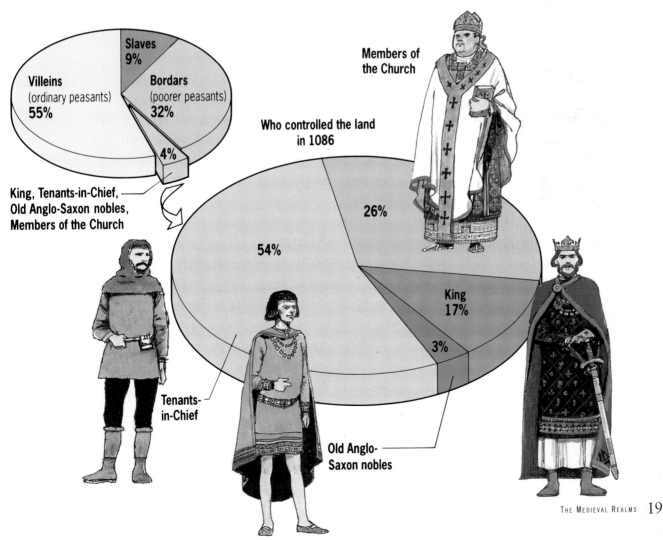

Villeins (ordinary peasants) 55%
Slaves 9%
Bordars (poorer peasants) 32%
4%
King, Tenants-in-Chief, Old Anglo-Saxon nobles, Members of the Church

Who controlled the land in 1086

Members of the Church 26%
54%
King 17%
3%
Tenants-in-Chief
Old Anglo-Saxon nobles

3.1 The Church and Christendom

The spread of Christianity.

Map legend:
- Christian i▮
- Christian i▮
- Islamic in
- Islamic by
- Islamic in but Christi... 1450
- Christian i▮ but Islamic 1450

Christendom

In the Middle Ages, Christendom was the name given to all the lands that were Christian. Look at the map above. Christendom was all the land coloured pink and red.

The Church and the Pope

The word 'church' comes from an Old English word meaning circle. 'Church' meant the whole circle of people who believed in Christ. The head of this circle, or church, was the Pope. He ruled over the Church.

The king

William the Conquerer was king of England from 1066–1087. He ruled England.

The king and the Pope – two bosses

People like bishops, priests, nuns and monks living in England had two bosses. The Pope was one boss. The king was the other boss. This could cause a lot of trouble.

A **William and the Archbishop**

William was a religious man so he and the Pope agreed about most things. William chose a Norman monk to be Archbishop of Canterbury. His name was Lanfranc. This was the most important job in the English Church.

SOURCE

Written by Nigel Kelly, a modern historian.

The king and the Pope – jobs

Many Churchmen, such as abbots, ran monasteries. They controlled a lot of land. The king wanted to be on good terms with them. Also abbots, bishops and other men in the Church were well educated. The king often asked them to help him run the country. The king tried to make sure that the bishops and abbots were men who would obey him. This did not always work.

King Henry I was crowned king in 1100. He and Archbishop Anselm argued over who gave out the jobs in the church.

B **William Rufus was king after William the Conqueror.** Tell the archbishop that I hated him yesterday, and I hate him more today, and I shall hate him even more tomorrow.

SOURCE

King William Rufus sent this message to Archbishop Anselm.

C Anselm made three conditions. First, the king must give back the land taken from the previous Archbishop of Canterbury. Secondly, the king must listen to his advice. Thirdly, the king must let Anselm obey the Pope.

SOURCE

From A.L. Poole, 'The Oxford History of England, Domesday Book to Magna Carta 1087–1215', 1951.

Questions

Read Christendom and The Church and the Pope.

1 Copy the sentences below. Choose one of the words in *italics* each time there is a choice.

All the people in Christendom believed in *Islam/Christ*. They all belonged to the same *Church/club*. Church comes from a word which meant *circle/square*.

Read Sources A, B and C.

2 Is the statement below true or false?

'William the Conqueror got on quite well with the Church. William Rufus did not.'

3.2 The Murder of Thomas Becket

Thomas and Henry II

In 1162, King Henry II made his friend Thomas Becket Archbishop of Canterbury. This was the most powerful job in the English Church. The king thought the Church would be on his side. But Becket put the Church first.

The row

The Church had its own law courts. Henry wanted just one set of laws and courts in England – his. Thomas disagreed. Henry and Thomas had a terrible row. In 1164, Thomas left England. But six years later he and Henry agreed to work together again.

Coronation

Henry wanted his son crowned king before Henry died. The Archbishop of Canterbury always crowned the new king. But Becket was not yet back in England. Henry did not want to wait. The Archbishop of York crowned the new king. When Becket reached England, he was furious. He sacked the bishops who had been on Henry's side.

Murder

Henry flew into a rage and is said to have cried: "Will no one rid me of this turbulent priest?" Four knights slipped away from Henry's court and went to Canterbury. Just after Christmas Day 1170, they murdered Thomas Becket in his own cathedral.

After the murder

Soon after the murder people began to say that people were cured when they visited the place where Becket was murdered. He was soon made a saint.

A **SOURCE**

They pulled and dragged him. They wanted to get him outside the cathedral to kill him, but he hung onto a pillar. They struck him and at the fourth blow spilt his brains and blood on the floor. He did not try to stop any of the blows and did not cry out.

Edward Grim, Becket's helper, describes Becket's death. It is probably meant to be Grim standing by the altar with the cross in Source B.

B **SOURCE**

A picture of the murder, drawn about 1200.

C

SOURCE

A picture of the murder, drawn in 1325.

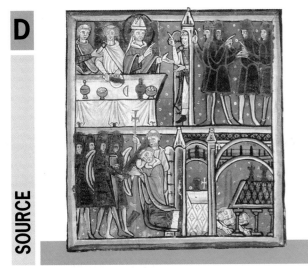

D

SOURCE

A picture from 1180. It shows the knights arriving (top), Becket's death (bottom left), and the knights praying later at his shrine (right).

E

SOURCE

A Dutch picture of the murder, drawn about 1480.

Questions

1 Read about the trouble between Becket and the king, and about the murder of Becket.

EITHER:

Draw a simple cartoon strip to show what happened to Becket from the time Henry II made him Archbishop of Canterbury until after his death.

OR:

Retell the story in your own words.

Look at Source B and Source D very carefully.

2 a Make a list of all the things that are the same in the pictures.

b Make a list of all the things that are different in the pictures.

> **Think about:**
> clothes, weapons, people, what the people are doing, where they are.

3.3 The Crusades

The Holy Land

Most people in Europe were Christians. But the land where Christ had lived was outside Europe. It was called the Holy Land. It was ruled by Muslims, not Christians. In 1095, the Muslims stopped Christians from visiting the Holy Land. Many Christians were angry.

The First Crusade

The Pope was the leader of the Christians. He asked kings, lords, soldiers and ordinary people in Europe to go and fight the Muslims. This war was called the First Crusade.

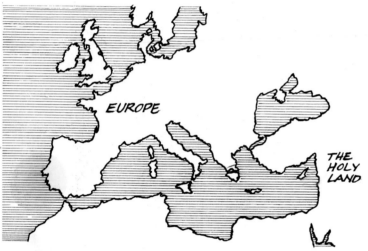

Europe and the Holy Land.

The crusaders capture Jerusalem

It was 1099. The crusaders captured Jerusalem, the most important city in the Holy Land. Some crusaders settled down to live in the Holy Land. But most crusaders went home. They thought they had won.

Other crusades

The Muslims fought back. Over the next 200 years, there were six crusades. Richard I of England led the Third Crusade in 1189. He was very brave and was given the name 'Lionheart'. Many of his battles were against the Muslim leader, Saladin. At different times the Muslims and then the crusaders seemed to be winning. But in the end, the Muslims kept the Holy Land.

A **SOURCE**

People who went to the Holy Land to fight were called crusaders. They wanted to capture Jerusalem, but some had other reasons. Some thought their sins would be forgiven if they fought. Others wanted land. Some knights were sent by kings who found them troublesome at home!

From 'The Medieval Realms', by Nigel Kelly, 1991.

B Saladin

SOURCE

Saladin devoted much of his time to drinking and gaming.

When he became ruler he took over other countries by force or trickery. This greedy tyrant then took the Holy Land.

An English monk wrote this about Saladin in the 13th-century.

A picture showing the siege of Jerusalem. It was painted in the 14th century.

D

SOURCE

Saladin was so determined to fight the holy war he thought of nothing else. He did not spend a single gold coin on anything else.

Saladin made sure that his men were fed and cared for. He never said bad things about people.

From a description of Saladin, written by a Muslim who lived at his court.

Questions

1 Copy the sentences below, matching the Heads and Tails.

Most people in Europe were	Muslims.
They believed in	Jesus Christ.
The Holy Land was ruled by	Christians.
In 1095 Christians were told not to	fight the Muslims.
The Pope said they should	called the Crusades.
These wars were	visit the Holy Land.

Read Source B and Source D.

2 a Write a sentence saying what the author of Source B thought about Saladin.

b Write a sentence saying what the author of Source D thought about Saladin.

3.4 Magna Carta

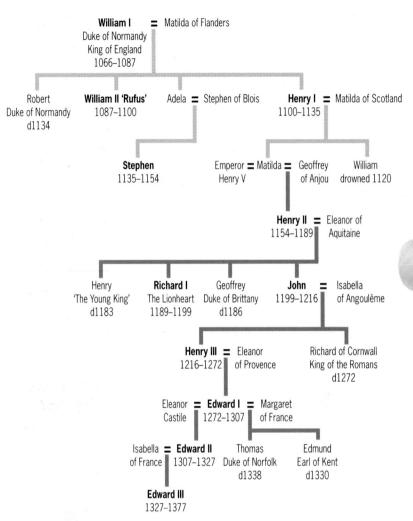

The Kings of England from 1066–1377.

A
SOURCE

He gnashed his teeth and rolled his eyes. Then he chewed sticks and straw like a lunatic.

A description of King John in a temper, written by a monk shortly after John died in 1216.

Magna Carta

I, King John, accept that I have to govern according to the law.

So I agree:

1 *Not to imprison nobles without trial*

2 *That trials must be in courts: not held in secret by me*

3 *To have fair taxation for the nobles*

4 *To let freemen travel wherever they like*

5 *Not to interfere in Church matters*

6 *Not to seize crops without paying for them*

… and lots more

The king

The king was important in the Middle Ages. A good king was strong. He was a good soldier. He was a good leader. He was fair. He made everyone obey the law.

King John (1199–1216)

King John was not a good soldier. He lost all the lands that England owned in France. English people did not like paying lots of money for John's armies, particularly when they lost.

What was John like?

John had a bad temper. He was cruel. He left the wife and son of one of his enemies to starve to death in prison. John loved good living and lots of feasting. He probably died from dysentry and overeating. But John had good points, too. He sat as a judge in many court cases and was often fair and kind to poor people. But he often did not obey the law himself and this made the great nobles and lords angry.

Magna Carta

By 1215 the great nobles had had enough. They banded together. They said the king must keep to the law himself. They made him sign the Magna Carta (which means Great Charter) to promise this.

Why the Magna Carta was important

The Magna Carta gave the rich nobles what they wanted. It also helped ordinary people. It was important because it tried to keep freedom for everyone in England.

Questions

Read the Magna Carta, which is on the scroll drawn on page 26.
1 Write the heading **Magna Carta**. Copy the sentence on the scroll that begins 'I, King John'

Read **Magna Carta** and **Why the Magna Carta was important**.
2 Why was it a good thing to get John to sign the Magna Carta?

3 Draw a picture to show one of the ways that King John would obey the law.

Read Source A.
4 Do you think that this is a fair description of King John?

> **Think about:**
> Who wrote it?
> When was it written?
> Does it sound likely?

B SOURCE

An embroidery, made in 1966, showing King John signing the Magna Carta.

3.5 Simon de Montfort and Parliament

Simon de Montfort

Simon de Montfort was a friend of Henry III. He married Henry's sister. But later Simon de Montfort quarrelled with Henry.

The Barons' Revolt

Simon de Montfort led the great nobles against the king. He won. For a while, Simon was the real ruler of England. While he was ruling he is said to have called the first parliament in England.

The Battle of Evesham, 1265

But the king fought back. Simon de Montfort was killed at the Battle of Evesham. The king had won.

Why call parliaments?

Kings always needed money. They had to pay soldiers and servants. They needed money to build castles. The best way to get money was to call a meeting of men from all the different parts of England. The king asked for money. The men often asked what the money was for. They talked and argued. Then they agreed to pay some money to the king.

A

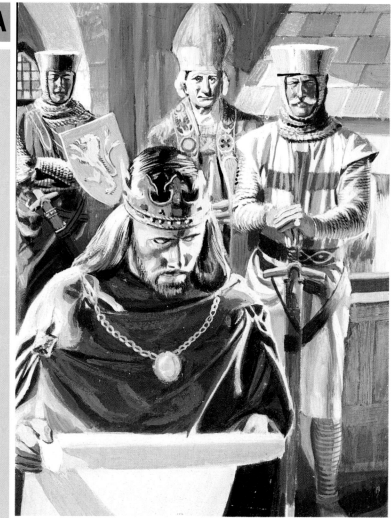

Simon de Montfort forces the captive King Henry III to call England's first real Parliament.

This Parliament is important because it is the first in which ordinary men were allowed to take part. It was called by a man named Simon de Montfort, and he not only called two knights from each shire [a county, like Kent] but also two citizens from each town.

SOURCE

From 'The Kings and Queens of England', Ladybird Books, 1968.

Men came to parliament from all over England.
Parliament comes from the French word 'parler',
which means 'to talk'.

From Great Council to Parliament

Kings had always asked their great nobles for advice. They wanted advice about going to war and raising money. When the king and his nobles met like this it was called the Great Council.

In 1215, King John was forced to sign the Magna Carta. From this time, kings **had** to ask the advice of the great nobles.

In 1265, Simon de Montfort called a parliament. This was made up of great nobles and ordinary men.

From 1300 onwards, kings called parliaments more often. Over hundreds of years parliament became stronger and kings became weaker.

Questions

Read **The Barons' Revolt**.

1 Fill in the gaps. Use the words in the box.
   Simon de _____ led the barons in a revolt against
   the _____. The barons won. For a while, Simon de Montfort
   was the real ruler of _____.

| king |
| Montfort |
| England |

2 Look at the pictures. Write a sentence for each picture, saying if it is
   a primary or a secondary source.

3.6 Henry II and Ireland

The Normans and Ireland

The Norman kings showed no interest in Ireland. They could see no point in trying to take it over, because it was a poor country.

Ireland in 1150

The people of Ireland had been fighting the Vikings for a long time. So Ireland was not very strong. There were many Irish kings and they fought each other. This also made the country weak.

Henry II and Ireland

In 1152, the king of Leinster (look at the map on this page) was Dermot MacMurrough. He fell in love with the beautiful wife of another king. He kidnapped her. There was a terrible row and a lot of fighting. Then Dermot asked the king of England for help. The king of England was Henry II.

Strongbow

Henry sent a Norman lord to help Dermot. The lord was known as Strongbow. Strongbow fought for Dermot and won. He married Dermot's daughter and was given lots of land in Ireland. This meant that he was growing powerful. Would he still be loyal to Henry?

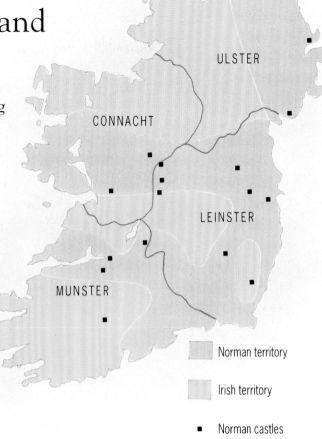

ULSTER

CONNACHT

LEINSTER

MUNSTER

Norman territory

Irish territory

■ Norman castles

A **SOURCE** Dermot was a man of warlike spirit, with a voice harsh from shouting in the din of battle.

Dermot MacMurrough described by Gerald of Wales. It was written at the time.

B **SOURCE** Some of John's friends laughed at the long beards of the Irish chiefs. They tugged their beards in a rude way.

Written by Gerald of Wales in 1186.

Henry goes to Ireland

Henry did not want Strongbow to be too powerful. So he went to Ireland. Henry forced the Irish kings to accept that he, Henry, king of England was their overlord. They had to promise not to work against him. Later Henry sent his son John to govern some parts of Ireland.

Questions

1 Copy the sentences below in **chronological** order. That is the order things happened.

   a Henry II went to Ireland.

   b Irish kings said they would obey Henry II.

   c Dermot asked Henry II for help.

   d Henry sent his son, John, to govern some parts of Ireland.

   e Strongbow fought for Dermot.

   f Henry sent Strongbow to help.

   g Dermot MacMurrough was king of Leinster.

   h Dermot fought another Irish king.

C **SOURCE**

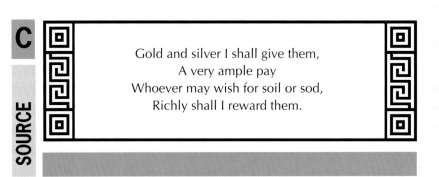

Gold and silver I shall give them,
A very ample pay
Whoever may wish for soil or sod,
Richly shall I reward them.

Dermot MacMurrough is said to have written this poem to get the Normans to help him.

Read Source A and Source C.

2 Copy out three of the words below which you think best describe Dermot MacMurrough.

gentle	brave
warlike	loving
lazy	rich
happy	loyal

D **SOURCE**

Trim Castle, one of the castles Henry II built to control Ireland.

> **Think about:**
>   What does he promise in Source C?
>   What does Gerald say in Source A?
>   What did Dermot do?

3.7 Edward I and Wales

William the Conquerer

William the Conquerer was always busy ruling England. He gave three of his Norman lords land on the borders or marches of Wales. (Look at the map on this page.) These three great Norman lords were called Marcher Lords. Slowly they conquered south Wales.

Llewelyn

Llewelyn was the powerful prince of Gwynedd. (His land is shown in yellow on the map on this page.) He refused to agree to take Edward I, king of England, as his overlord. So, in 1277, Edward sent three armies to attack him.

Llewelyn in the mountains

Llewelyn retreated into the mountains around Snowdon. Edward ordered his soldiers to camp around the mountains. They stopped any food getting to Llewelyn's armies. Soon Llewelyn had to surrender. Edward allowed Llewelyn to stay and rule Gwynedd. But a few years later Llewelyn rebelled again. He was killed and his brother David was hanged, drawn and quartered.

A SOURCE

David was hanged, drawn and quartered. His body was sent to four parts of the country. His head was sent to join Llewelyn's at the Tower of London.

From D. Richards and A.D. Ellis, 'Medieval Britain', 1973.

B SOURCE

400 masons
1,000 labourers
200 carters
30 smiths and carpenters
all worked to build Caernarfon. Stone blocks were brought by sea.

From a report sent to Edward I in 1296.

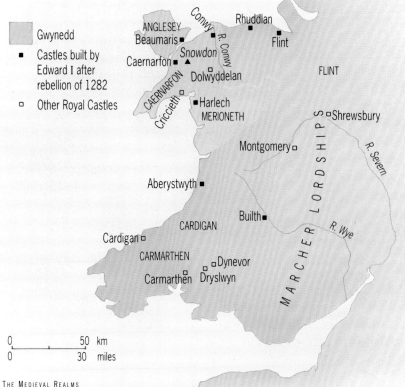

Gwynedd

■ Castles built by Edward I after rebellion of 1282

□ Other Royal Castles

Rhuddlan
Conwy
ANGLESEY
Beaumaris
Snowdon
R. Conwy
Flint
Caernarfon
FLINT
Dolwyddelan
CAERNARFON
Criccieth
■Harlech
MERIONETH
Shrewsbury
Montgomery
R. Severn
Aberystwyth
MARCHER LORDSHIPS
Builth
R. Wye
CARDIGAN
Cardigan
CARMARTHEN
Dynevor
Carmarthen Dryslwyn

0 ___ 50 km
0 ___ 30 miles

The castles that Edward I built in Wales. The counties named here were created by Edward in 1284.

C

SOURCE

Beaumaris Castle, built in 1295.

Castles

Edward wanted to make sure that the Welsh did not rebel against him again. He needed to make sure that he could control them. Edward built lots of big, stone castles in Wales. (The map on page 32 shows these castles as black squares.)

Prince of Wales

Edward also tried to please the Welsh. In 1301, he made his eldest son Prince of Wales. This was to make them feel that their country was important enough to be ruled by the most important of the king's sons.

Questions

Read **William the Conquerer**.
1 Write a sentence to answer each of the questions below.
   a Why was William too busy to conquer Wales?
   b Who did William give land to?
   c What were these Norman lords called?
   d What did these lords start to do?

Look at the map on page 32. Read Source B.
2 a How many royal castles were built after 1282?
   b How many people do you think would have been needed all together to work on these castles?

3.8 Robert Bruce and Bannockburn

Edward I invades Scotland, 1296

Edward I wanted to rule Scotland as well as England and
Wales. He captured the Scottish king and said that from
now on Scotland was part of England.

Edward – Hammer of the Scots

As soon as Edward was back in England, the Scots
rebelled. Edward had their leader William Wallace,
hanged. All was quiet for a while.

Robert Bruce

It was 1305. Some Scottish lords secretly crowned Robert
Bruce, king of Scotland. But Bruce had no castles and no
army.

*A picture of Edward I with his
first wife, Eleanor. This was
painted at the time.*

B

SOURCE

C

For as long as one hundred of us remain alive we shall never submit to English rule.

SOURCE

From a declaration by Scottish lords, made in 1320.

The Great Seal of Robert Bruce, made in 1326. This side shows him as a warrior. The other side shows him as a king.

Edward I dies

In 1307, Edward died. The new king was Edward II. He hated battles and fighting. Quickly, Bruce captured castle after castle in Scotland. At last Edward II felt he had to do something. He marched to Scotland.

Battle of Bannockburn, 1314

Bruce defeated Edward II's English army at Bannockburn, near Stirling in Scotland. A few years later, the new English king, Edward III, agreed that Scotland was free.

While he was hiding from the English, Bruce watched a spider at work. A legend has grown up around this.

As Bruce was hiding in a cave, he saw a spider try and try again to make a web. The spider showed Bruce that he must try and try again to be king of Scotland.

Questions

Read **Edward I invades Scotland** and **Edward – Hammer of the Scots**.

1 Copy the sentences below. Choose one of the words in *italics* when there is a choice.

Edward I wanted to rule *Scotland/France* as well as England and Wales. He captured the Scottish *thistle/king*. But when he went back to England the Scots *rebelled/cheered*. He had their leader *clapped/hanged*.

Look at Source B.

2 Choose three words from the list below that you think best say how the artist saw Bruce.

fat   clever
brave   warlike
shy   heroic

4.1 Medieval Warfare

Big battles

The Battle of Hastings, where William the Conquerer beat the English, was a big battle. Most fighting was not like that.

Sieges

A lot of fighting happened around castles. An army camped outside a castle did all sorts of things to try to break in. They used battering rams, catapults and rocks. They dug under the castle walls. Castles were very difficult to break into until gunpowder was invented.

Burning and killing

A lot of fighting was made up of burning farms and villages and killing the people who worked there. This meant that enemy soldiers would have no food to live on.

Tournaments

Tournaments were competitions which tested the fighting skills of the knights and the foot soldiers. They lasted for about four days. They were a way for soldiers to practise fighting. Most of the fighting was between two people, not big groups. Sometimes fighting at tournaments was to the death. But the king did not like this because it killed off useful soldiers.

Richard I's coat of arms on his shield.

Two knights jousting at a tournament.

A

A picture of the Battle of Crécy, which happened in France in 1346. It was painted a long time after the battle. The French fought the English. The French are using crossbows. The English are using longbows. The English won.

Knights

Knights rode horses. They could move fast. They could ride over people on foot. But there were not many knights in an army. This was because horses were expensive.

Foot soldiers

Most soldiers fought on foot. Archers used long bows. Other soldiers used swords, axes or pikes. Pikes were about three metres long.

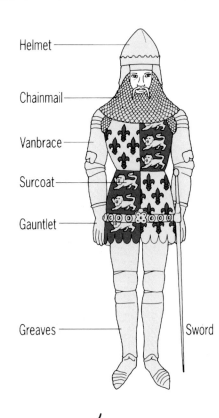

Helmet

Chainmail

Vanbrace

Surcoat

Gauntlet

Greaves — Sword

A medieval knight's armour.

Questions

Read **Big battles**, **Sieges** and **Burning and killing**.
1 Write the heading: **Fighting in Medieval Times**.
   Write one sentence about each of these ways of fighting.

Look at Source A. Look at the drawing of a knight's armour.
2 Draw a picture of knights jousting. It can be as simple as you like, but try to show the armour clearly.

4.2 Crime and Punishment

The king wanted everyone to obey his laws. Then all the people in England could live in peace. Sometimes people did not obey the law. They stole or murdered. The king said they must be punished.

Religion and ordeal

Everyone believed in God. They believed God would punish bad people. They believed that God would help good people. So they often let God decide.

Ordeal by fire

A man might be accused of stealing some money. He had to carry a red hot iron in his hand and walk three steps. His hand was badly burned. If the hand had gone bad in three days, God was saying that the man had stolen the money.

Ordeal by water

A woman accused of witchcraft might be tied up and thrown in a river. If she floated she was a witch because the river (and God) had rejected her. If she sank she was innocent. But if she sank she died anyway!

The Jury system

Henry II set up more courts with juries. In these courts the judge (often the king) and the jury listened to evidence about whether a person had committed a crime or not. Then they decided whether to punish him or not.

Punishment

Many crimes such as murder were punished by death. Ordinary people were hanged. Rich people were beheaded.

Mutilation

Cutting off parts of the body was common. A person who stole a purse might have his or her hand cut off.

A

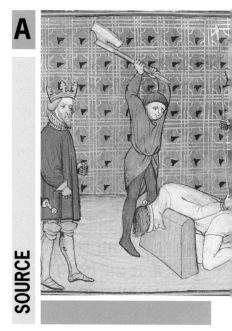

Having your head cut off was a quick way to die.

B

Being hanged was a slow way to die.

The execution of Earl Waltheof, 1077

Waltheof sobbed so much he could not finish saying the Lord's Prayer. So the executioner cut off his head anyway. Then the head finished the prayer.

A description of the execution, written about 60 years later.

D

People were put in the stocks for a day for crimes like selling bad meat. Other people threw rotten food or mud at them.

Questions

Read **Religion and ordeal**, **Ordeal by fire** and **Ordeal by water**.

1 Copy the sentences below. Choose one of the words in *italics* each time there is a choice.
Everyone believed God would *punish/help* bad people. They often let God *decide/hide*. They used ordeal by *fire/feasting* and ordeal by *wishing/water*.

2 Copy the table below. Fill in the punishment you think would have been given.

Criminal	Crime	Punishment
Tom the peasant	Stealing money	
Lord John Ridd	Murder	
Old Mary	Being a witch	
John the butcher	Selling bad meat	

4.3 Religious Beliefs

God

In Medieval times, everyone in Britain believed in God. God was all powerful. People who believed in God also believed that Jesus Christ was the son of God. He lived in about 1 AD. These people called themselves Christians.

Christians

As the years went by many people became Christians all over Europe. They all believed in God and the Devil, and in Heaven and Hell.

Salisbury Cathedral was begun in 1220. It took 38 years to build.

The Church

The word 'Church' comes from an old English word meaning 'circle'. All Christians belonged in this circle. Many early churches were built in the shape of a circle. So church came to be the word used for the building Christians met in.

Heaven and Hell

Christians believed they would go to Heaven if they were good. They would go to Hell if they were bad. Some people became monks or fought in the Crusades to show they were giving up their lives to be good and love God.

Questions

Read all the paragraphs.

1 Fill in the gaps. Use the words in the box.

In Medieval times everyone in _____ believed in _____. They thought that Jesus Christ was the _____ of God. These people were called Christians. They were all part of the same _____. The word 'church' comes from an old word for _____.

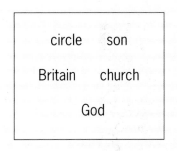

circle	son
Britain	church
God	

Look at Source B. It shows Jesus sitting in Heaven. Angels sent people to Heaven or Hell. Good people went to Heaven. Bad people went to Hell. Church walls often had pictures like this on them.

2 a Write a sentence to describe Hell.

b Write a sentence to describe Heaven.

Think about:
Is it calm?
Is it painful?
It is forever.

B

SOURCE

A medieval painting showing people being sent to Heaven or Hell. It was painted in 1430.

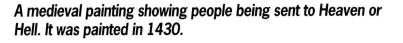

4.4 *Life in a Medieval Monastery*

Monks and nuns

Monks lived in monasteries. Nuns lived in female monasteries or nunneries. These monks and nuns gave their lives to God. Many lived in monasteries with very strict rules. These rules were written by a monk called St Benedict.

What they gave up

Monks and nuns gave up everything.
1 Their names. They had to choose new ones.
2 Their families and children.
3 Their land, houses, animals, chairs, tables, fine clothes and money.

What they promised

Monks and nuns promised three things.
1 To be poor.
2 To be good.
3 To be obedient.

Studying and writing

Monks wrote out books. They decorated them with beautiful pictures. It took a long time. Some monks and nuns ran schools.

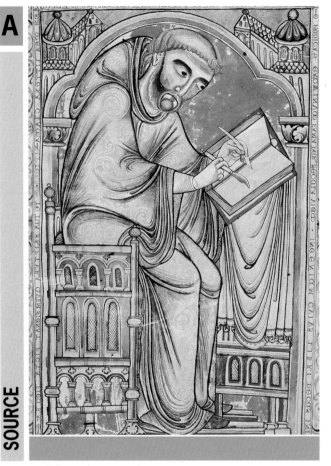

A

A monk copying a book by hand. It took months to copy one book.

B

This monk looked after the food and drink in a monastery.

Farming

Monks grew food for the monastery. Some rich people gave land to monasteries. These monasteries sold wool from their sheep or wood from their forests, and were rich.

Praying

The monks and nuns prayed a lot. Rich people sometimes asked monks and nuns to pray for them.

C All monks shall work in the kitchen.
All monks should work on the farm or in holy reading.
A mattress, woollen blanket and pillow is enough for bedding.

SOURCE

From the rules of St Benedict.

D

FOR BREAD, MAKE A CIRCLE WITH BOTH THUMBS AND THE NEXT TWO FINGERS.

FOR HONEY, PUT OUT THE TONGUE AND TOUCH YOUR FINGERS AS IF YOU WISH TO LICK.

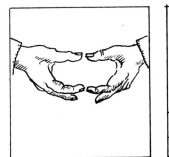

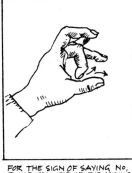

FOR THE SIGN OF SPEAKING, HOLD THE HAND AGAINST THE MOUTH AND SO MOVE IT.

FOR THE SIGN OF SAYING NO, PLACE THE TIP OF THE MIDDLE FINGER UNDER THE THUMB AND MAKE IT SPRING BACK.

SOURCE

Questions

Read **Monks and Nuns**.

1 Copy the sentences below. Choose one of the words in *italics* each time there is a choice.
Monks were men who lived in *huts/monasteries*. Nuns were women who *visited/lived in* nunneries. They spent their *afternoons/lives* serving God. They had to obey *strict/easy* rules. These rules were written by a monk called *Brian/Benedict*.

Read **What they gave up**.

2 Draw a cartoon to show what people gave up to become monks and nuns. It can be a very simple drawing.

Read Source C.

3 a What work did monks do?
b What bedding did they have?

Signs of Silence

Many monk and nuns were not allowed to talk. They used sign language. Here are four of the sorts of signs that they used.

4.5 Life in a Medieval Village

Farming

Most people were farmers. They grew wheat to make bread. They harvested it and ploughed the land. They kept chickens, geese, pigs and cows for food.

The Lord of the Manor

The Lord of the Manor was a rich man. (Often he was the under-tenant, see page 13.) He owned all the land in the village. The peasants or villeins worked for him. They farmed his land. He would let them use strips of his land to grow things for themselves in return for the work they did for him.

The reeve and the villeins

The reeve worked for the Lord of the Manor. The Lord gave land to the reeve as payment for the work the reeve did. The reeve's job was to make sure that the villeins worked hard. He had to make sure that they all worked together.

SITUATION VACANT

Required 1 Villein

Must be prepared to:
1. Pay taxes to the Lord
2. Work on the Lord's land for up to twelve days a year.
3. Never leave the village or let his children be married without the Lord's permission.
4. Agree to grind all his corn in the Lord's mill. (and pay a fee)
5. Not to catch rabbit, deer or any other animals in the wood (they belong to the Lord)

VILLEIN'S CAFE
TODAY'S MENU

Breakfast: Served at dawn. Dry bread & watery ale.
Lunch: served at midday. Bread, a little fish or meat & watery ale.

Supper: served at dusk Thick vegetable soup bread, fresh fruit watery ale or cider.

SPECIAL
if available
MILK
CHEESE
EGGS

A SOURCE

A reeve supervising work in the fields.

B

February: ploughing. Sources B, C, D and E are all from a 14th-century calendar.

C

April: sowing.

The villein's hut

The villein and his family lived in a hut. The hut was just one small room. It had no windows. The floor was made of mud (often mixed with ox blood to make it set hard). The pigs, chickens and other animals lived in the hut too.

D

July: harvesting.

Questions

Read the paragraphs on page 44.
1 a Who owned the land on the manor?
  b Who farmed the land on the manor?
  c Who made sure that they did this properly?

Look at Source A and Source D. They both show harvesting.
2 a Who is the man with the stick in Source A?
  b What is the same in both sources?
  c What is different in both sources?

E

December: pig killing.

4.6 Life in a Medieval Town

Towns were small in the Middle Ages. But they were very busy places. Everyone came to the towns to buy and sell things.

A Medieval town. ▲

Market day

Farmers' wives walked or rode to the market town. They sold butter, eggs and cheese. Farmers sold cows, sheep and pigs in the market.

Who bought from the farmers?

Butchers bought cows, sheep and pigs. They killed them and sold the meat in their shops.

Bakers bought eggs and wheat. They made cakes and bread to sell in their shops.

Everyday shops

There were many shops in a town. Some shops sold food. Others sold goods like saddles and leather goods for horses, or clothes and candles. Each shop had a sign to show what it sold.

A Medieval shop sign. ▼

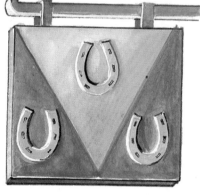

Shops and apprentices

Many people worked at home. So, a shoemaker bought pieces of leather. He made them into shoes in his backroom. Then his wife and children sold the shoes from the front room or shop. A busy shoemaker had apprentices working for him. Each apprentice worked for the shoemaker for seven years to learn how to be a good shoemaker.

A

SOURCE

A 15th-century wall painting. It shows a medieval shop.

Guilds

All the shoemakers in the town had to belong to a guild. The guild had strict rules. This was to make sure that there were not too many shoemakers in a town. Also that all the shoemakers made good shoes. There were guilds for many other trades too. Potters, barrelmakers, weavers, clothmakers, bakers and butchers all had guilds too.

Questions

Look at Source B and the drawing of a town on page 46.

1 List the things that are different.

2 All the surnames below come from the names of jobs in Medieval times. Use a dictionary to find out what the jobs were.

Tanner	Fuller
Mason	Cooper
Fletcher	Potter

3 Design a shop sign for one of the jobs in question 2.

A walled Medieval town. From a 14th-century manuscript.

4.7 Women in Medieval Times

Monks and history books

Most people could not read or write in the Middle Ages. Monks were some of the only people who did learn to read and write. So monks wrote the only history books we have. They wrote about men and what men did.

Women and history

But women made up about half of the population. What did they do? We do not know very much about women because the monks did not write much about them. We only know about queens or women who did 'men's jobs'.

What could women do?

One of the reasons that the monks did not write much about women was because women were stopped from doing many jobs. Women were not allowed to have important jobs in the Church. They were not allowed to vote in parliament, or to help run the country. When Henry I tried to make his daughter, Matilda, ruler after him it started a civil war (see Source B).

B SOURCE

Queen Matilda

Matilda was the only surviving child of King Henry I, so he said she should rule when he died. But many nobles did not want a woman ruler. Henry's brother, Stephen, took over. There were 19 years of fighting over the crown.

C SOURCE

Eleanor of Aquitaine

Eleanor was Countess of Aquitaine. As a woman she had to marry, even though she was rich. She married King Henry II of England.

A SOURCE

Joan of Arc led the French soldiers into battle against the English. She was allowed to do this because people believed her when she said God had told her to do it.

Women's lives

Most women got married and had children. They looked after their families. They often worked on farms. They also worked at different crafts, like spinning wool. Some helped their husbands to run shops. And if a woman's husband died she carried on the business. A cloth merchant's widow might carry on buying and selling cloth.

A woman milking a cow.

A woman making a net.

A woman blacksmith.

Questions

Read **Monks and history books**.

1 Fill in the gaps. Use the words in the box.

Few people could read or _____. Most history books were written by _____. They wrote about _____.

> men   write
> monks

Look at the picture sources.

2 Which show women doing 'men's work'?

4.8 Medicine

Women and medicine

Most people could not afford to pay a doctor. The women in the family often cured everyday sicknesses by using herbs they grew in the garden or picked in the hedgerow. Many modern medicines come from herbs. Willow was said to help headaches. Aspirin comes from willow.

Doctors

Doctors were mostly men. They had studied medicine. But people in Britain at the time did not know much about how the body worked.

War

There were many wars, so doctors learnt how to treat wounds. They learnt to seal wounds with a red hot poker. But patients often died of shock! Often wounds went bad.

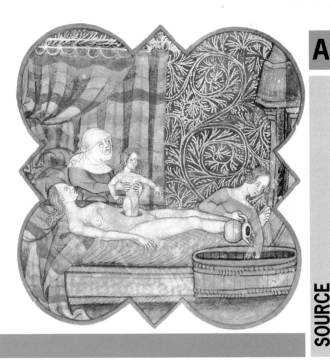

A

SOURCE

A woman surgeon doing a caesarian operation. Many women died after an operation like this. Very many women died having babies.

B

SOURCE

C I know you have many doctors. Remember what Pliny had written on his tombstone: 'I died of too many doctors.'

SOURCE

A letter written to the Pope in 1350.

A 13th-century picture. This shows Edward the Confessor making a person well by touching them. People thought kings could do this.

God's anger

Some people felt that illness was a sign of living a bad life. They thought that God was angry with the sick person. They said that if this was the reason you were sick then it was wrong to help to make you better. The sick person just had to wait until God decided they had suffered enough and made them well again.

The doctor in this picture is taking blood out of a patient. Many illnesses, especially high temperatures, were said to come from having too much blood.

SOURCE

Questions

Read **Women and medicine** and **Doctors**.

1 Copy the sentences below, matching the Heads and Tails.

Many people could not pay for	herbs as medicine.
The women of the family used	studied medicine.
Many modern medicines	men.
Doctors were people who had	the way bodies worked.
Doctors were mostly	come from herbs.
But they did not know much about	doctors.

Read Source F and **God's anger**.

2 a How would medieval people treat an illness that came from God?
  b How would medieval people treat warts?
    Do you think everyone in the 20th century would say this was wrong?

E Take a candle and burn it close to the tooth. The worms that are gnawing the tooth will fall out.

SOURCE

A medieval cure for toothache.

F Even today there are wart charmers. They make warts disappear. Medieval people thought it was sensible. They believed good spirits cured the person.

SOURCE

From a history book published in 1976.

4.9 The Development of the English Language

How English came about

Over hundreds of years many different people invaded England. They all spoke different languages. Slowly the languages mixed together.

Middle English

By the 1300s, many people spoke Middle English. It was a mixture of all the languages that had come from different invasions. Look at the modern sentence below and where the words have come from.

A silly monk who was visiting his friend let the pigs out. The pigs got through the gate and fell into a bog.

silly	Anglo-Saxon
monk	Latin
visiting	French
friend	Anglo-Saxon
pigs	Middle English
gate	Norse
fell	Anglo-Saxon
bog	Gaelic

A **SOURCE**

A woman from Kent was puzzled when a man asked her for eggies. She called eggs eyren.

This is a story that was told by the printer, William Caxton.

B **SOURCE**

She was so charitable
  and so piteous
She wolde wepe, if that
  she saw a mous
Caught in a trap.

From 'The Canterbury Tales', written by Geoffrey Chaucer in the 1380s.

How to make 'Middle English Soup'
Ingredients:
Gaelic
Anglo-Saxon
Latin
Norse
French
Method. Add each ingredient to the pot one at a time and stir very slowly until well mixed up.

People spoke differently in different places

By 1476, most people in England spoke Middle English. But people from different places in England had very different accents.

Printing

William Caxton started to print books in 1476. Most of them were written in Middle English. This encouraged more and more people to speak Middle English. Printing books was much quicker than writing them by hand. So many more books were made.

Questions

Read **How English came about** and **Middle English**.

1 Draw a cartoon of a cooking pot to show how the languages got mixed up. Try mixing up the letters too.

2 Make a list of the modern words below. Write next to each word the country you think we may have got the word from.

Pizza	Lager
Hamburger	Tandoori
Spaghetti	Vindaloo

Look at Source C.
3 How does the source show that some people thought that books were important?

Think about:
   How Caxton feels.
   How the king feels.

C SOURCE

William Caxton printed this picture of himself giving a book to Edward IV in 1477.

5.1 The Black Death – the Plague Arrives

The Plague arrives

It was June 1348. A French ship came sailing into a little English port. The port was Melcombe, in Dorset. The ship tied up and the sailors unloaded the goods on to the quay. Then they went off into the town. But one sailor was ill. He had the plague and soon died. But others had already caught the plague from him. They passed it on to other people. The plague spread very quickly. No one knew how it spread. No one knew how to cure it. Everyone was scared they would catch it next.

Bubonic plague

The plague was the deadly bubonic plague. It got its name from the buboes (lumps) that swelled up on people's bodies. The buboes were usually in places like the armpits. The big swellings turned black before a person died. So the plague was called The Black Death.

 SOURCE A

Some of the planets are close together. It is a terrible sign.

Written by a doctor in the 14th-century.

SOURCE B

God has sent the plague to our town because people gamble and fight.

Written by someone living in Leicester in the 14th-century.

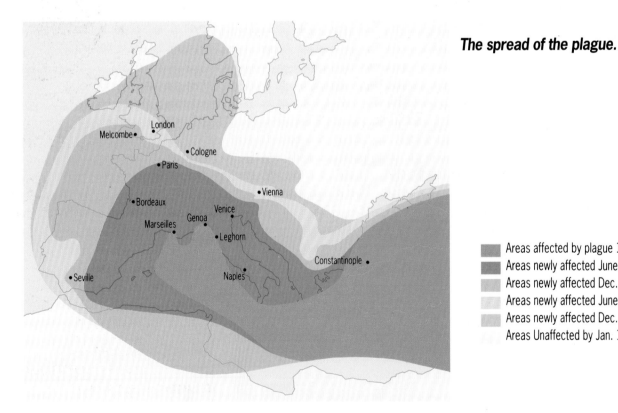

The spread of the plague.

Areas affected by plague 1347
Areas newly affected June 1348
Areas newly affected Dec. 1348
Areas newly affected June 1349
Areas newly affected Dec. 1349
Areas Unaffected by Jan. 1350

How many died?

No one is quite sure how many people died of the Black Death. Most historians think that between one third and one half of all the people in England died.

SOURCE C

A priest praying for plague victims.

Questions

Read **The Plague arrives**.

1 Look at the pictures on this page that show how the plague spread. Draw a cartoon to show how the plague arrived. Show:

- The French ship arriving.
- The crew unloading the goods.
- The crew leaving the ship.
- The sailor passing on the disease.
- The sailor dying.
- The plague passing on.

> **Think about:**
> What else left the ship at the same time as the crew?
> How did the plague spread?

How the plague spread.

5.2 The Black Death – Effects

How many died in 1348 and 1349?

No one is sure how many people died. But at least one third of all the people living in England died. Some historians think that as many as a half of all the people in England may have died.

Villages and farms

Sometimes whole villages died. Every house was empty. Cows and sheep wandered in the streets. There was no one left to look after them.

More freedom

Some people did not catch the plague. They were lucky. There were lots of jobs for them. They could ask for more money for ploughing and looking after animals. Many villeins said they would only work for lords if they were given freedom and more money.

A SOURCE

When it was time for the rent to be paid no one came from the village of West Thickley. They were all dead.

From D. Richards and A.D. Ellis, 'Medieval Britain', 1973.

B SOURCE

This churchyard is specially consecrated to bury plague victims. There are more than 50,000 bodies here.

Written in 1349 in Spittlecroft Churchyard, London.

Percentage of priests dying from the Black Death.

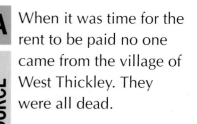

Exeter	Winchester	Norwich	Ely	Lincoln	York
50%	49%	49%	48%	44%	39%

The Statute of Labourers, 1351

Parliament passed a law. It said that villeins could not have more money. They could not be free. Lots of lords and villeins ignored the law. People who had survived the Black Death were not frightened by parliament.

A picture from 1349. It shows plague victims being buried in Tournai, in the Netherlands.

C SOURCE

Questions

Read **Villages and farms** and **More freedom**.

1 Fill in the gaps. Use the words in the box.
Sometimes everyone in the _____ died. Every _____ was empty. Some people did not catch the _____. They could ask for more _____ for working on the farms.

> house   money   village   plague

Look at the diagram of the percentage of priests who died. Priests held church services and visited the sick.

2 a Which town has the highest percentage of deaths?

b Which town has the lowest percentage of deaths?

c Write a sentence saying why you think a higher percentage of priests died than ordinary people.

The Peasants' Revolt – Why did it Happen?

YOUR JOB IS TO WORK FOR ME.

The peasants were fed up with everyone telling them what to do.

The Poll Tax

Richard II wanted more money to pay his soldiers. He was fighting France. Richard said everyone over the age of fifteen years must pay him a tax. It was called the Poll Tax. Many poor peasants were very angry. In 1381, there were riots when King Richard's men started to collect the tax. This was the start of the Peasants' Revolt.

A

SOURCE

It seems to me that these evil times are the result of the sins of the people of the earth.

Written by a monk at the time.

B

SOURCE

Every man and woman must work for the same wages as before the plague.

From The Statute of Labourers, 1351.

C

SOURCE

We condemn villeins who won't work for their lords like they used to.

From an Act of Parliament passed in 1377.

King Richard's Poll Tax Demand

All men shall pay the following:

(Married men shall also pay for their wives)

1 In the year 1377   4d

2 In the year 1380   4d

3 In the year 1381   12d

All men resisting are to be thrown in prison.

By order of the King

D

SOURCE

My friends, the state of England cannot be right until everything is owned by all the people together and there is no difference between nobleman and peasant. We must tell the king we are badly treated.

From a speech made by John Ball in 1381.

E

SOURCE

Peasants will not live on stale vegetables and cheap beer. They want fresh meat or fish.

The views of some of the peasants.

F

SOURCE

A picture of John Ball leading some peasants. They are carrying the royal flag to show they are loyal to the king.

Questions

Look at the scroll on page 58.

1 a How much poll tax did a man have to pay in 1377?

  b How much poll tax did a man have to pay in 1381?

  c How much poll tax did a man have to pay for his wife?

Read Source B.

2 How do you think the peasants felt about The Statute of Labourers?

Read Source D and Source E.

3 a What would you think the peasants wanted if you only had Source D?

  b What would you think the peasants wanted if you only had Source E?

  c You have both. What do you think the peasants wanted?

> **Think about:**
> Why do you think people did not like the Poll Tax?

5.4 The Peasants' Revolt – What Happened?

Wat Tyler

It was the summer of 1381. The peasants were angry. Wat Tyler was a strong leader. He led the angry peasants. They did not want to pay the Poll Tax. They wanted villeins to be free.

To London

60,000 angry peasants marched to London. King Richard decided to meet the peasants. First he met the peasants who had marched in from Essex. The king promised to do what the peasants wanted.

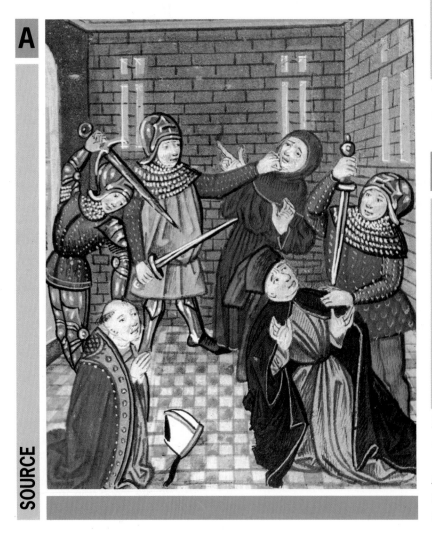

A SOURCE

B SOURCE

Richard asked the peasants what they wanted. They said: 'We want you to set us free forever'. Richard said he would.

From a chronicle written in 1381.

C SOURCE

Oh you wretched men, detestable on land and sea. Villeins you were and villeins you shall remain.

Thomas Walsingham's version of what King Richard said, 1381.

D SOURCE

Tyler stabbed the mayor. The mayor drew his sword and struck back. He cut Tyler on the neck and head. Then one of the king's followers ran Tyler through with his sword, killing him.

From a chronicle written in 1381.

A 15th-century painting of the murder of the Archbishop of Canterbury.

SOURCE E

A picture of the Death of Wat Tyler. It is in two parts. On the left Richard watches the murder. On the right he goes to the peasant soldiers after the murder.

Death of the Archbishop of Canterbury

But the peasants from Kent were violent now. They broke into the Tower of London. They murdered the Archbishop of Canterbury.

Tyler killed

The king met the peasants again. This time one of the king's men killed Wat Tyler. The angry peasants turned on the king. He shouted to them: "Sirs, will you shoot your King? I shall be your leader and you shall have what you want."

Going home

The peasants went quietly home. But the king did not keep his promises. Some of the peasant leaders were hanged. None of the peasants were any better off.

End of the Poll Tax

However, King Richard never dared put on a Poll Tax again. And over the next 100 years peasants and villeins became free from their lords.

Questions

Read **Wat Tyler**. Write a sentence to answer each of the questions below.
1 a What kind of a man was Wat Tyler?
  b Who did he lead?
  c Why were the peasants angry?
  d What did the peasants want?

Read Source D. Look at Source E.
2 a List the things the sources agree about.
  b List the things the sources disagree about.

5.5 The Wars of the Roses

Lancaster and York

There were two powerful families in England in 1454.
Both families were descended from Edward III.
Both families thought they should rule England.

Lancaster (red rose) and York (white rose)

The two families chose different signs to put on their
badges. People used the badges to show who they
supported. Both sides chose a rose. The people who
supported the Lancaster family chose a red rose. The
people who supported the York family chose a white
rose. So the battles between them were known as
the Wars of the Roses.

The two families started to fight in 1461. First one
side won. Then the other side won. (Look at the
map on this page.) While everybody was fighting it
was difficult to run the country.

Battle of Bosworth Field, 1485

Finally, Henry Tudor (Lancaster) killed
Richard III (York) at the Battle of
Bosworth Field in 1485.

The Tudors

Henry Tudor became King Henry VII. He was the
first Tudor king. At first people thought he would be
beaten in a battle. They thought the fighting would go on.
But Henry was not beaten. He ruled well. He made sure
that the lords and great men did not get too powerful.

The battles of the Wars of the Roses.

Hexham 1464

Towton 1461

Wakefield 1460

Blore Heath 1459

Ludford 1459

Bosworth 1485

Mortimer's Cross 1461

Tewksbury 1471

Northampton 1460

Edgecote 1469

1455
St Albans
1461

Barnet 1471

LONDON

Lancastrian victory

Yorkist victory

HENRY IV
1399-1413

HENRY V
1413-1422

HENRY VI
1422-1461

LANCASTER

YORK

HENRY VI

EDWARD IV 1461-70

HENRY VI 1470-71

EDWARD IV 1470

1471-83

HENRY VI murdered 1471

EDWARD IV

Edward V
1483

?

HENRY TUDOR

RICHARD III 1483-1485

becomes

RICHARD III
killed at the Battle of Bosworth Field.

HENRY VII
1485-1509

ELIZABETH
of YORK

both Houses united by marriage

Questions

1 Copy the sentences below, matching the Heads and Tails.

Two families fought over   red rose.
The Lancaster badge was a   who should rule.
The York badge was a   King Henry VII.
In the end Henry Tudor became   white rose.

Look at the map on page 62.

2 List the battles that the families of York and Lancaster fought in **chronological** order. That is the order they happened.

INDEX